What Does a Cowboy Do?

by Jesse Blackwell

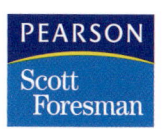

PEARSON
Scott Foresman

Editorial Offices: Glenview, Illinois • Parsippany, New Jersey • New York, New York
Sales Offices: Needham, Massachusetts • Duluth, Georgia • Glenview, Illinois
Coppell, Texas • Sacramento, California • Mesa, Arizona

cattle

cowboys

Who Is a Cowboy?

A cowboy is a person who works with cattle. There were many cowboys long ago in the American West. Today, there are still some working cowboys.

There are women who work with cattle, too. They can be called cowgirls.

Cowboys feed the cattle and take care of them.

What Does a Cowboy Do?

A cowboy or cowgirl does many kinds of work with cattle. They take care of the cattle. They ride horses to round up the cattle. Cowboys take cattle to market. At the market, the owner sells the cattle.

---

round up the cattle: to gather the cattle together and move them along

trailer

What Is a Cattle Drive?

Long ago, cowboys rode horses and herded cattle along trails. This is how ranchers got their cattle to market to sell them. Sometimes it was a long trip that lasted for weeks. It was called a cattle drive. Now cattle are taken to market in trailers pulled by trucks or in trains.

hat
bandanna
chaps
spurs
boot

What Do Cowboys Wear?

A cowboy's clothes help protect him from the weather. Most cowboys wear blue jeans, shirts, boots, and hats. The boots may have metal parts called spurs. Some cowboys wear leather chaps to cover their pants. Many cowboys wear bandannas. Cowboys may also wear gloves to protect their hands as they handle the ropes.

rope

What Tools Does a Cowboy Use?

A cowboy needs a saddle to ride his horse. A saddle is a seat on a horse's back. A cowboy also needs a rope to catch cattle. Today, many cowboys drive trucks to carry food for the cattle.

hat

police officer

Is Everyone Who Wears a Cowboy Hat a Cowboy or a Cowgirl?

Many kinds of people like to wear cowboy hats. Some singers wear them. People in movies wear them. Police sometimes wear cowboy hats. Boys and girls sometimes wear them. Would you ever like to wear a cowboy hat?

barrel

What Is a Rodeo?

A rodeo is a contest where cowboys and cowgirls show their skills. The events include horse riding, barrel racing, and more. A rodeo is one place to see cowboys and cowgirls in action. What would you like to see a cowboy or cowgirl do?